PROJECT

FLSirmans.com is a Website created and maintained solely by Freddie L. Sirmans, Sr. himself. It is very informative. It has many links that are not endorsed by the writer himself, but are added to help and serve you.

Freddie L. Sirmans, Sr. Keeps his own counsel, he asks no one, but he is an avid reader and news watcher. He knows ninety percent of his writing will go over most people's heads and will not be understood because of his outdated judgment and deep, deep wisdom.

He gladly tells you what you will never hear from the mass media. The fact is simple, if you have never read Freddie L. Sirmans books, you don't really know what is taking place in this great country. It's a fact; history has and will continue to prove him right.

No one seems more unqualified to sound the alarm of the coming avoidable collapse than him, but destiny has reached out and grabbed him for a call to duty.

To refuse is not an option to him; it doesn't matter if he has poor language skills, being uncomfortable around people, somewhat antisocial, neurotic, and on and on. He doesn't know why his raw, crude, uncut message must go forth regardless? But, it must for the sake of US. And western civilization survival.

Sure, he feels
some wholesale book dealers are not stocking and are blackballing his books, but an idea whose time has come can't be held back it must prevail.

Many are quietly buying bootlegged Freddie L. Sirmans books, but will never admit it in public because they think he is some kind of right wing kook or nut.

However, he learned years ago that those that can genuine love and forgive others don't go crazy, do evil deeds, or fail in life. He would rather give his life than to hurt or embarrass his family and decent people.

In his view the most selfish act of all is to take ones self out and take someone else along. No one can be one hundred percent sure what a human mind will do, but in his experience those that are selfish and unforgiving are the most prone to act out something violent and evil.

One must believe in someone positive or something positive bigger than self, otherwise the world will revolve around self and self-serving may become the only thing that matters.

All blame then becomes someone else's fault. And if you couple that with unforgiveness, then you may have a ticking human time bomb on your hand. The ability to forgive and count your blessings always works to relieve depression and is the foundation of the Christian religion.

The big, big open secret that no one will face and everyone is running away from is mind and mood altering legal drugs.

In almost all cases of individuals committing horrendous mind-boggling crimes the individuals were hopped up on some legal depression drug, but it is ignored out of existence. As to the young, kids has played doctor and experimented from the dawn of history.

You show me yours; I'll show you mine is not new. But now, kids are out of control and treated like adult and given a written criminal record for life, when all is needed to set them on a straight and narrow right course is a sugarless diet and some painful licks on the behind.

The only thing wrong with this great country is the welfare state, and no matter what anybody thinks, privatizing out of it is the only thing that's going save this great country. As for gun control, don't fool yourself, almost all liberal politicians want it, they are just lying low and hiding their intent, but waiting to pounce when they think they can get a kill. The real underlying reason the liberals really want to ban the gun doesn't have anything to do with crime.

They want to make this welfare state the sole authority in this country for a complete take over, and that can't be done as long as we have an armed populace. Western Europe is too far-gone, the US. With its armed populace is the only thing saving individual freedom for the masses in the world today.

For years the liberals in this country had their way by using their free candy store and promoting the "course of least resistance," but not any more.

With talk radio and other sources more and more people are on to them. People are realizing that conservative and religious values must be restored before it is too late.

When it comes down to raw survival, conservatives have and will always win in the end. That is why talk radio won't work for liberals. No one wants to hear blame, blame, blame, and excuse after excuse.

Decent and responsible people expect everyone to be responsible for their own

YOUR ECONOMICAL SURVIVAL BIBLE

actions, case closed. Hallelujah. Give God the praise.

I always say that I'm uneducated. What I really mean is I'm not formal educated above a high school grad. Sure, for technical and other specified fields a formal education is a must, otherwise people that read are the most informed and intelligent that you can find.

I fall in the fairly well read group and that is mostly limited to non-fiction. Even as a kid I have always enjoyed reading.

One of the best things any parent can do for their child is to reward them for reading books, especially poor and low-income kids. It may be the only thing that will break the chain of myths and ignorance passed down from many generations.

I heard at a very young age that I would never amount to anything. If not for my love of reading I could possibly be locked away somewhere in some insane mental ward.

There was a time when I dreaded going to sleep at night because of terrible nightmares. Then I read a book on the "The power of positive thinking" by Dr. Norman Vincent Peale. That book gave me the faith that "I could do all things through God which strengthens me." And I haven't had a nightmare since and that whole scenario took place over forty years ago.

STIMULUS, STIMULUS, DUMB, DUMB, I THINK!

To me a stimulus package is like putting paper money down a rat hole. All it does is make a bad situation worse. When a nation is spending almost twice as much as it is taking in it is insane to think more spending is the answer, it is impossible to spend your way out of debt.

I truly understand how an economy works and to me the answer is very simple. The first truth is government spending is the problem and until that is recognized and admitted there is no saving the USA and global economy. What congress and the president needs to do first right now is recognize that this nations survive is at stake and act accordingly.

Instead of going on silly financial wild goose chases, void all regulations on businesses right now. Next, completely eliminate the minimum wage. Next, set up temporary emergency government run commissaries, government run housing in all these empty buildings, government run clinics, and using tokens or script for all who qualify for these government services.

Next, stop all government spending except
for military and essential government only
functions. I know to most this line of thinking
will be
seen as insane, but, I assure you the
stimulus path will lead to guarantee doom for
the USA, or we end up as a debt slave owned
and controlled by foreigners.

My way to salvation is only a suggested path
to take it doesn't have be word for word like I
say but the path is a way out of no way, a
word to the wise should be sufficient. God
bless America.

PS: This path will set the USA economy free
and guarantee without a shadow of doubt
that entrepreneurs and the free market will
save this great nation with freedom intact,
nothing else can do that.

We must place all of our faith and trust in the
proven ideology of the "Free market place at
work.
**SIRMANS LOG: 1 SEPTEMBER 2011, 0846
HOURS**

**IS HURRICANES THE WRATH OF AN
ANGRY GOD?**
The ancients certainly thought so and came
up with human sacrifices and all kinds of
appeasements. Believe it or not, however,

excluding the sacrifices there are still some that fall prey to that type of thinking.

Myself, to that type of thinking I say poppycock, hogwash, bullcrap, or some other tits on a boar hog like metaphor. It is all nonsense, what goes around comes around and that includes the works of Mother Nature. It also includes the working of every economy, too.

Every economy has a boon and bust cycle and sooner or later the bust cycle is going to come back around no matter how much scheming and fine tuning the egg heads does. That is just a fact of life.

So, when we become dumb and stupid and let the welfare state replace and destroy our bread and butter nuclear and extended family system that leaves us up S... Creek without a paddle.

Today when most people first read my writing they think I must be some kind of extreme right wing kook or loon that is out of touch. What they don't realize is one hundred years or so ago 95 percent of Americans though as I do.

The validity of a strong nuclear and extended family system with good morals and values haven't changed in five thousand years; it is we who have changed for the worst as a people since the "New deal" birthed our welfare state.

When the woodchopper gave up on trying to split a mighty oak block before walking away he decided to knee down and take a closer look. And sure enough he could barely see it but there was a tiny beginning split. He realized all of his long hard effort had not been totally wasted.

I feel the same as the great wood chopper, except after all these years of my writing effort I still can't see any reward, I wish I could just quit and walk away and never look back, but, I know I must carry on as long as any life left in me. I guess if I can enlighten just one person it will have been worth it. **SIRMANS LOG: 30 AUGUST 2011, 1135 HOURS.**

OMG! JUST WHAT I NEED! THE IRS!
I placed all of my faith in TurboTax for the last few filing years. Now, here comes the IRS hot on my tail and closing in fast. Hopefully, I will live and survive to write another day.

I'm not complaining I'm a big boy now, I can take it; I just hope I escape with my hide and not be skinned alive. Seriously, if its determine that I owe I will pay, I may be too proud to beg but I'm not too proud to pay. I have active duty served my country and will

always gladly do my citizens
duty.

As a writer, maybe some humor can be found
here; I have shared so much about my life,
why close my life book on this. God bless and
keep this great nation always.
**SIRMANS LOG: 23 AUGUST 2011, 1806
HOURS.**

GOD BLESS OUR FEDERAL RESERVE!
This idea of getting rid of the Federal Reserve
is just plain dumb and stupid. That is like
saying get rid of the government. You can't
have an organized society without
government.

There must be a government to protect and
safeguard the whole society. However, what I
am against is a welfare state type of
government, which I believe is
unconstitutional. Without government means
anarchy with every man for himself.

The same thing applies to the economy;
there must be some type of organized money
system. Otherwise, you are left with only
trade and bartering to survive. These people
talking about getting rid of the Federal
Reserve are just plain ignorant, it is the best-
organized money system
known to man.

What type of currency to use is left up to congress and the president? Maybe its time congress and the president consider getting back to a genuine physical currency with its value in the currency itself. But, to seriously consider getting rid of the Federal Reserve is shallow and short sighted.

What are you going to replace it with, a feudal system with Lords and castles, I think not. Right or wrong that is my one man's opinion.
SIRMANS LOG: 21 AUGUST 2011, 0730 HOURS

FOOD STAMP'S DESTRUCTIVE POWER!
I place food stamps as the third most destructive force behind the "New deal" and the minimum wage to a genuine free market place economy.

Number one is the "New deal" when it started giving free unearned money to the poor. Sure, the poor must be helped as a last resort and not allowed to starve. But, if the free market place is to survive the government must never give out free unearned money to anyone.

The only way the government can help the poor and disadvantage without destroying the free market place is by temporary establishing government run commissaries, housing, and clinics. And even that should be done only as a last resort after the extended family, the church, the community, and all else has failed.

Otherwise government will replace a survival need for the nuclear and extended family and in time the nuclear family will cease to exist. The reason why that will in time kill every economy is because there are only two players in an economy; they are a seller and a buyer or merchant and consumer.

The government is only a necessary parasite needed to protect the whole society. Government has the power and the big guns and many times takes over and run the whole show, but only a free market place economy can feed its entire population.

In a free country if government would just stay with collecting taxes, protecting the country, and doing only what the people can't do for themselves the economy would police itself and produce far more than the population could use.

Mother Nature's supreme law of "Natural selection" would maintain a natural balance between the buyers and sellers and purge out inefficiency, moral decay and other anti-survival forces. But, when government takes its tax money and gives out on an individual basis free unearned money and food stamps to the poor that creates enough people with the money to keep higher and higher priced merchants in business.

Then the government raises the taxes on the higher and higher priced merchants and the merchants passes their extra cost on to the public in a never ending inflationary spiral. After the "New deal" and the government started giving out free unearned money on an individual basis that ignited inflation but by then government had tasted the God like power of being a super provider.

Then the die was cast and I don't believe big government ever intend to give up one inch of its cradle to grave God like great white father provider role come hell or high waters. When it comes to money it is not the amount that truly matters it is the buying power that really counts.

Once inflation kicks in higher taxes on merchants only means higher prices passed on to the public. I didn't research when the minimum wage was started but at some point government decided the minimum was a good idea, I totally disagree.

All the minimum wage does is remove the safety valve from a free market place economy, it is then like a vehicle with no reverse or a hot water heater with no pop off valve. Folks, now don't get me all twisted I know the things I criticize was genuine intended to help the poor and to a lesser extent get politicians elected.

I know food stamps was meant to be a good thing but just like free unearned cash it is deadly destructive to a free market place economy when given out on an individual basis.

With government not giving out free money to the poor It is impossible for most merchants to charge more than the poor can pay and stay in business because there is never enough rich to keep commerce flowing. When government is not involved in the free market place that will keep the cost of living down to where the people can pay their on food and doctor bills.

When government do help the poor and disadvantage by establishing government run commissaries, housing, and clinics it should always use tokens or scripts. That will make sure government spending is kept separate and not contaminate the nation's economy in any way.
SIRMANS LOG: 17 AUGUST 2011, 1245 HOURS.

LAST CALL TO ELIMINATE THE MINIMUM

WAGE!

The egg heads, the ruling class, and the elites all think I'm some kind of nut case that few knows about and I should be ignored out of existence, wrong.

When I keep harping on completely eliminating the minimum wage they think I'm a fool and don't know what I am talking about, wrong. Eliminating the minimum wage is the only thing that is going to save western civilization by starving the welfare state beast out of its all-powerful super provider role.

That and that alone can set the free market place free to save western civilization. Nothing else can do it. That act alone will permit the nuclear and extended family system to rebound along with good moral and plenty of emergency life sustaining bartering capacity. Otherwise, if we fail to eliminate the minimum wage western civilization is done.

It will very soon have zero chance of surviving. The reason is Mother Nature herself is going to use its supreme law of "Natural selection" to reset western civilization back to zero, in other words the Stone Age.

The welfare state has destroyed 90 percent of the foundation that holds every society together. And without the elimination of the minimum wage the welfare state will complete the job with 100 percent destruction. I'm talking about a 100 percent destruction of the nuclear and extended family system.

As to good ethics and morals, right now we have men marring men and women marring women and before long good ethics and morals will be something found only in the history books. And the old standby of having adequate emergency backup bartering capacity in case the economy fails, meaning many, many small farmers and home gardeners, they are now like so many, sucking on the welfare state provider tit.

Just in case anyone is thinking that if things get out of hand martial law will be used to demand order by force, could be in for a rude awakening. At this point western civilization without eliminating the minimum wage soon won't have any foundation left to support civilization or an organized society.

That being the case no amount of authority can prevent total chaos back to the Stone Age. Only the elimination of the minimum wage can save what little that is left of a foundation to survive on and reverse course before going over the cliff and taking western civilization with it.

Of course, I know I will be ignored more than ever but I believe my great supernatural wisdom is God given. Go ahead a laugh and dismiss me as a bigger nut than ever, but, one thing is for sure "We all dance to the tune of a distance drummer." Glory be to God.

The real secret is, life is all about maintaining a balance, and I know most of my views are too one sided and to the extreme, but only drastic thinking and actions at this late stage can create a middle balance.

Once the minimum wage is eliminated the next step is the government must never give out free money to help anyone on an individual basis. To help the poor, needy or anyone the government must establish temporary commissaries, housing, and clinics and use tokens or script for those that qualify.

That will prevent government spending from igniting inflation and destroying the free marking place like what is killing today's economy. I assure you sooner or later some nation is going to see the light and grab my no minimum wage lifeline wisdom, not every one is going to play Russian roulette with their nations' survival.
SIRMANS LOG: 07 AUGUST 2011, 0011 HOURS

"OOPS! THERE IT IS!"

Like I've said before, the liberals will see you in hell before they will cut spending and stop the growth of government. For whatever reasons, those pushing for the collapse of the USA and global economies, it may be all down hill from here.

I knew it, I knew it, the conservatives and others would not be able to withstand the pressure, now I guarantee you taxes are going to be raised on the fewer and fewer businesses left standing. Lord knows I hope I'm wrong on this, but I'm afraid this may be the final nail in the coffin before the sunsets of the USA and global economies.

Like a broken record I'm still at it on pleading for the eliminating of the minimum wage. I yell to the world this welfare state beast is out of control and is just too powerful and mighty. But like David with his stone and slingshot I promise you, the elimination of the "Minimum wage will bring this beast to its knees and put the people back in control over their government.

Nothing else is going to break its death grip on the USA and global economies. The dam is about to burst, and once the dominos start falling no one knows where it's going to end, it may be back to the Stone Age, only God knows, God save America, Amen.

SIRMANS LOG: 02 AUGUST 2011, 1455 HOURS

THE FORGOTTEN, ONLY GUARANTEED PENSION!

What this entitlement generation has forgotten or don't even know is for over 5000 years your only survival pension was your children.

Until around eighty years ago when the "New deal" and this monster size welfare state came about the nuclear and extended family system allowed civilization to exist for over 5000 years. It is not a perfect system but no society have ever survived and existed without it in the history of mankind.

In the USA except for maybe a few veterans almost no one was on the government dole before the "New deal" came along. Sure, in the beginning social security was a good thing for the elderly and the severely disadvantaged, but now every body and his brother is on it.

Those that put all of their faith in government don't know history; there has never been a government that didn't go broke at some point. To let this big government welfare state kill the nuclear family system by taking away it survival need like what is happening is not only dumb and stupid it is sheer madness.

Never put all of your survival eggs in one basket, especially a tax hungry out of control welfare state beast. The biggest problem now is the welfare state has produced so many dependents so long that nearly 40 percent of the population has no clue as how to survive using self-initiative.

I wish somebody would please show me how in the hell you are going to pay your way out of debt by going deeper into debt, like the liberals are trying to do.
SIRMANS LOG: 30 JULY 2011, 2025 HOURS.

MASS ECONOMIC IGNORANCE!
About 95 percent of the American people's knowledge of how an economy truly works can be compared to a little kid that believes grits and eggs come only from the grocery store.

Even most economist has bought into this liberal garbage claptrap entitlement mentality that started with the "New deal." But, I'm here to tell you there are no free rides in life somebody always pays.

All wealth originates from some type of trade or business transaction by the private sector, period. No wealth originates from government it is always taken from somebody or somewhere. The first rule in economic is "You can't get blood out of a turnip."

You can't eat money and if there are not enough people producing food there is going to be starvation no matter whom the liberals blame. When a
nation prevents the private sector from making a profit it cuts its own throat that is biting the hand that feeds it.

Only a free market place nation can create wealth and feed its entire people, all other economic systems leads to mass starvation, that is the history, you can look it up. But, when have a liberal ever had common sense, very seldom in my view.
SIRMANS LOG: 29 JULY 2011, 0859 HOURS

WELFARE STATE DEATH GRIP MUST BE BROKEN!
As I set back and watch all of the ado going on about raising the debt ceiling I just take the whole thing with a grain of salt. In the grand scheme of things it really doesn't matter if they raise it or not because all that is doing is buying just a wee little more time.

Either way it is not going to stop the welfare state from killing off both the USA and global economies. As a supposition example, if miraculous all of the USA's debt and financial problems were solved today, we as a nation will still be doomed.

The reason is money and lack of jobs are direct and obvious, but the real things that hold every society together is not so obvious and have rotted away to the very core because of the welfare state. Number one, the base and foundation for all human survival are the nuclear and extended family system.

Nothing can exist and be strong without a survival need, and the welfare state has took away that need for the strong nuclear family and left this great nation with no means to survive when the going get rough, and believe me tough times is just over the horizon. And the other two critical survival means of good morals and adequate emergency backup bartering capacity are practical nonexistence.

I know no one want to hear it, but I repeat again and again that the only thing that is going to save the USA and western civilization is the complete elimination of the minimum wage as a start. Nothing else can break the death grip the welfare state have on this nation's economic throat; otherwise the welfare state is going to finish off the kill.
SIRMANS LOG: 23 JULY 2011, 0005 HOURS

INFLATION'S BIGGEST MYTH AND MISCONCEPTION!

The biggest misconception about inflation is that the mass printing of money by government is the cause of inflation, wrong. Government can print all of the money it wants to and that alone will not ignite the cost of living consumer inflation.

So, OK, the government prints up all of this worthless money? But, in order to ignite inflation it has to get that money to enough people on an individual basis to corrupt the natural balance between the merchant and the consumer. Handing out free unearned money on an individual basis that and that alone is the cause of the cost of living consumer inflation.

That is why I keep screaming so loud that government should never give out free unearned money on an individual basis. Sure, as a last resort when the nuclear and extended family, the church, the community, and social organizations all fail then government must come to the rescue.
And even then government should help the poor by establishing government run commissaries, housing, and clinics, and using scrip or tokens to prevent destroying the USA national economy, which has happened.

Now, about 80 years after the "New deal" and mass false shallow liberal thinking it is just the opposite with close to 95 percent of the American people looking to government as the first resort for survival help, Lord, what a shame. But, oh, no, my great God given wisdom is totally ignored; I don't believe the eggheads will ever detour from the gimmick laden economical course of least resistance we are on today.

SIRMANS LOG: 16 APRIL 2011, 1631 HOURS.

WILL OBAMACARE SURVIVE?
UPDATE: 23 JANUARY 2011, 1243 HOURS.

What I see and understand so clearly on how an economy really work is simple, yet it shocks me why so few get it. Now almost everyone is focused on medical insurance, who got it, who can't get it, and on and on.

The Lib's rammed this Obamacare down our throats and believes that is the magic answer. I think all of that is missing the root problem with paying for medical care in America.

The root problem with medical care in America is "The lack of market forces due to the Federal government involvement." That involvement created the deadly side effect known as "Ultra-high-cost."

So, that makes "Mr. Ultra-high-cost" the real true villain in medical care. The government itself can't pay ultra-high-cost and 90 percent of the American people can't pay ultra-high-cost.

All any insurance company does is collect enough money from a lot of healthy well people and bet not too many of them will become sick at any one time.

Insurance companies won't have the money if more than just a few of their customers become sick at a time, which means they can't afford "Mr. ultra-high-cost."

So, the shallow minded liberals decided they would solve the whole problem by forcing every able body adult to pay for medical insurance or go to jail, which I think is a dictator tactic, and un-American.

They figured that would produce enough healthy well people paying into the system to satisfy "Mr. ultra-high-cost," and in theory that should work. But, that can never work when not enough people have jobs. Then it all boils down to the bottom line.

Before any business can make one red cent of profit or pay one employee's salary it first must pay a yearly business license fee, permit fees, federal income taxes, state income taxes, local option taxes, social security tax, unemployment tax, Medicare tax, state sales taxes, and taxes I can't even think of, plus satisfy all kinds of government red tape mandates.

Oh! I had forgotten to include having to make rent or mortgage payments too before the first penny of profit is made. I can't remember the statistics on the survival rate of all new startup businesses, but I think it is less than three percent still standing after five years.

On top of all of that everybody including the healthy young people is going to be hit with a new big whopping Obamacare health care tax.

Then and only then after paying all of that a business must try to find enough profit left to pay the employees, restock, take care of utilities, do maintenance and then live off what is left, it is no wonder why there are no jobs. Plus, some utility companies piles on by charging a business almost twice the rate that they do the public.

I believe when the Obamacare impact fully hits the jobless rate is going to sky rocket even higher than it is now, and then you add all of the welfare state dead beats, that is a lot of people not paying into the system.

If Obamacare survives I just don't think there are going to be enough people paying into the system even if they do start giving the old folks pain pills and sending them on their way.

In fact at this stage I know beyond a shadow of doubt that eliminating the **"Minimum wage"** and kicking the welfare state out of its social and family provider role is the only thing that's going to save the USA.

The family provider role must be restored back to the head of household where it belongs and where it always was until the "New deal" came along. That must be done or this great nation perishes.

Everyone keep griping about not making a living wage, but I will guarantee you that is a losing battle because the bigger the government the farther the cost of living out distances a living wage, there is no getting around that fact.

The only way to solve that is to get the government to stop giving out free money on an individual basis. If that is done the cost of living will have to come down to where poor people can pay their own medical bills and other cost, simply because the government will no longer be subsidizing and driving up prices.

Without the government subsidizing high prices by giving out free money on an individual basis very few merchant can charge more than the poor can pay and stay in business.

Sure, the government should help the poor and not let anyone starves, but does that by setting up temporary commissaries, kitchens, shelters, clinics, or whatever.

But, don't destroy the county's free market place, its culture, and everything else by giving out free money on an individual basis, that is what ignited the killing inflation that is eating us alive today.

Right now no one wants to hear my no **"Minimum wage"** solution, but they will, just wait, its coming, mass starving is right around the corner, you'll see.

Come on folks! Y'all got eyes and a brain! What goes here? Sometimes I wonder if the liberals really are this economically ignorant or just want go ahead and push this great nation on over the cliff. They are still speeding up government spending instead trying to cut back.

I know it's unthinkable, but what if they are trying to force martial law for a once and for all absolute government take over, government already owns 90 percent of the real estate market and big chunks of the manufacturing industry. Maybe I'm crazy to think out loud like this. Lord have mercy on my soul.

Using tunnel vision and looking at survival one dimensional through the economy prism only is the deadly mistake most egg heads and ninety five percent of the population are making.

All, even a real physical currency does is make trade and bartering a zillion times more convenient. Civilization has never survived only on faith and I don't believe it can today, and paper money is just that.

Civilization can and did survive on trade and bartering long before money was invented, but no society or nation is going to survive very long without all four legs of the survival stool holding strong, otherwise the nation will soon fall from within.

You can call it culture or whatever, but I see the first leg of the four legged survival stool as a strong nuclear and extended family system. The second leg I see as a strong moral and religious code in place.

The third leg I see as adequate bartering capacity backup in case the economy fails. That requires many small farmers and home gardeners, and with no citizen expecting the government to guarantee their survival.

And the fourth and last leg I see as the economy with a stable currency. Now, if anyone thinks we in the USA have a stable currency, good for you, I'm not so sure.

Being able to see all four legs of what I believe is the survival stool in perspective I think raises me above the tunnel vision and one dimensional thinking that so many so called smart people fall prey to.

Again, I write what I think, I don't try to tell anybody what to think, I might be a snake oil salesman myself for all you know. Do your own thinking and check more than one source.

If you don't see any validity in what I write just continue writing me off as a nut case and believe what the liberals tell you. Thank you for taking the time to read this article, and may God bless you. With love always, yours truly, bye.
SIRMANS LOG: 20 JANUARY 2011, 1736 HOURS.

THE POWER OF JUST SAYING "NO!"
Never under estimate the power of just saying "NO." Nancy Reagan said it years ago about using drug and everybody laughed and

said that was too simple, but what people fail to realize is it really works; of course nothing works in every single case.

I'm here to tell you the power of just saying "NO" is awesome when it stands alone, adding anything else just dilutes its effectiveness. Plus, when used in tandem as "Positive thinking" it is one awesome power. I am one that has long believed in the power of the "Positive thinking" technique.

It is a technique where one takes a quote or saying and repeats the same thing over and over to ones self fifty or more times a day to change behavior. I'm telling you just say no to whatever you don't want to do and it works, of course everyone has a free choice to over rule, but, to just say "NO" works.

For example, if I want to be a Vegan, all I need to do is just say: "No animal fat." Nothing else needs to be said, it works. Example#2, If I want to stay away from white flour, I just say: "No white flour" and that's it, it works, just say "NO."

If you are eating too much at mealtime, just repeat to yourself when needed: "No big meals," nothing else needs to be said, it works.
SIRMANS LOG: 14 SEPTEMBER 2011, 1220 HOURS.

WORLD GREATEST STRESS RELEIVING AND HEALING QUOTE!

QUOTE: "I can wish all people goodwill through God which strengthens me." One can leave off the through God which strengthens me or substitute in place of God ones own deity.

Just repeat the quote to yourself as many times as necessary or until the storm passes over. No one else has to know what you are repeating to yourself.

I promise you if you have trouble on your job, in your marriage, or whatever, your stress will vanish, it is not a cure all, but, a stress free healing process will began.

True joy and happiness comes from within. But, you can't find it from within. You find it by caring, helping, and serving others!

DIABETES HELPFUL HINTS

Every diabetic should read labels and keep count of the amount of carbohydrates consumed. Carbohydrates are really what determine ones blood sugar level. If carbohydrates can be kept down to around 50g per meal it will go a long ways in controlling ones blood sugar level.

Meats and fats without anything added like sauces and gravies don't contain carbohydrates. Most leafy vegetables and others like greens beans, broccoli, cauliflower, and sweet peas average around 15g per 1/2 cup. It is the big 5 that can be enjoyed but really need to be kept under control, they are bread, rice, potatoes, pasta, and artificial sweets.

My healthy eating priority formula: Eat, fresh and raw when possible, cooked fresh, cooked frozen, and lastly cooked canned. However, as a rule eating food properly cooked is always safer in my view. I'm not a trained medical professional in any way; I'm a self-made writer and hope my limited knowledge will be helpful to someone in some way.

USA AS GLOBAL ECONOMIC SLAVE!

Government as a super social and family provider means economic suicide when given enough time. It's simply impossible to make it work in economic terms. So far we have manage to get away with it since the "New deal" but the Jig is up, natures supreme law of "Natural selection" has finally chased us down and we are gonna pay dearly.

An economy has only two players a seller and a buyer and "supply and demand" is what they operate on. It doesn't matter how

modern, complicated, or big an
economy is that is still the process that
makes any economy work over the long haul.
A free market place that allow free
competition is the only system know to man
that
has never failed to always produce an over
abundance of everything.

With a minimum wage and mountains of red
tape the USA is no longer even in the
Ball Park in terms of a free market place
economy. Government is not part of an
economy but is a necessary parasite needed
to safeguard and protect the whole
society.

The people started off trading and bartering
and evolved into using a currency to
buy and sell. Generating a profit is the
lifeblood that drives every successful
economy. Profit is what government takes in
the form of taxes and is what allows
government to exist.

Our government was designed to take only
enough profit to safeguard and protect
the nation, but the "New deal" opened up a
small gate into a provider swamp. Now
around eighty years later floodgates are wide
open leading into a giant government
provider swamp. Government is taking more
and more profit in the form of higher
and higher taxes and has become a full-

fledged super provider from cradle to grave.

With this going on it will be impossible not to
suck any profit generating economy dry,
we are done, cooked and ready to be served.
This is why plead so hard for people to
see the wisdom of completely eliminating the
minimum wage, the free market place
is the only thing that is going to feed us and
keep us alive. Big government and red
tape got a strangle hold on the USA economy
and it can never be broken as long as a
minimum wage is in place.

Ninety five percent of the USA population
can't see pass the amount of money. Its
nonsense to thank in terms of a thousand
dollars when thirty years ago a dollar
would buy more, it is the same with a
minimum wage, it just make things unreal
and distorts the whole economy, get rid of
the minimum wage and it will save us from
total doom.

Only as a last resort the government must
help the poor but it should never give out
free money on an individual basis that
destroys the natural balance between the
merchant and the consumer and drives
inflation out of sight like we have today. The
only way government can help the poor and
not destroy the main economy is to
provide government run kitchens, housing,
and clinics and use tokens or script.

That way the economy will be kept in balance and the nation can then afford to repair the infrastructure and everything else like before the "New deal." Unless my advice or something like it is taken the country and whole infrastructure is going to unravel in the not too distance future.

The eggheads are not going to change, if the people don't take the bull by the horns and vote out these liberals soon we all are going to be at each other's throat. I will repeat, if the minimum wage is not eliminated and the red tape slate not wiped clean the USA will end up as a slave to the global economy in my view.
SIRMANS LOG: MAY 31, 2011, 1637 HOURS

GUN TO HEAD CARD SWIPE!!!
The credit card swipe fee is a good example of free market thinking, which very few truly understand today. As a committed free market thinker I believe the government should just butt out of the whole credit card swipe fee matter, but I know it won't.

Good intentions are always subjective and not free market thinking. A banks survival depends on making a profit, but the retailers that is charged the swipe fee is not forced to pay the fee. So, what is the problem with that? There is no gun to the retailer's head making him use the service.

That is a balance between a buyer and a seller and it will always work itself out and seek a natural level if the government just butts out. The retailer can pass the cost on or just completely refuse to participate. The retailer can give cash discounts for paying cash or unlimited ways to deal with the situation.

But, in the end the banks can never charge more than the free market place can bear and stay in business. It is government control that distorts and destroys a natural balance between the buyer and the seller. With government involvement what can happen is fewer and fewer bank will offer customer friendly innovated card services in the future.

I have no gripe either way. I consider myself just a free market place thinker and not a judge or jury either way. But, the trend and norm today is to do the right thing and be fair which in the end always creates inefficiency and excessive waste.

SIRMANS LOG: JUNE 8, 2011, 0851 HOURS

PEOPLE TAKE NOTES!
NEW ENTRY: 27 JUNE 2011, 1159 HOURS

Here I go self-aggrandizing again, but, if it get through to just one thick scull to me its worth it. Here I am a poor uneducated phobia ridden insecure neurotic South Georgia USA country boy writing on the world stage, only in America.

I don't know where my great wisdom comes from; it must be destiny or a gift from God. It's not normal, I don't know if its supernatural or what, all I know is it is real, and somebody better listen. There I said it, you can dismiss me as a nut case, right wing kook, nut, loon, or pick your choice of words, but you won't logically prove me wrong.

Enough said, now lets get down to brass tacks, I don't know or have never read any of the great economic thinkers, everything I say about economic is ninety nine percent my own creative thinking. Everything I know about learned economic thinking is derived from a pamphlet I read about thirty-five years ago that said "All economies starts with bartering."

My great mind took that statement and can now dissect an economy with perspective that fits it into the over all grand design of human survival. I don't believe anyone can truly understand economics unless they have a basic understanding of how nature works.

The first law in understanding nature is to know that all survival is based on cycles otherwise there could be no existence. No matter what, real or imagined, if it didn't have a die or rebirth cycle it would crowd out the entire universe.

So, the thing about an economy and everything else in existence, no matter what system, it is designed by nature to collapse at some point. Sure, man with knowledge can manipulate and extend the collapse time for an economy, but the greater the extend time the greater the effect.

Before modern time the boom and bust cycle was around every seven years but the effect was small and the Nuclear and extended family system, the strong religious and moral code, and emergency backup bartering capacity with many small farmers and home gardeners just took over until the rebirth boom cycle kicked in again, and the following bust cycle was mostly a nuisance.

Nothing has really change the cycle is just a lot longer and it may take us back to the stone age if we don't rebuild a strong nuclear and extended family system. So, I hope you see, in terms of overall human survival there are thing far more important than just the economy, civilization survived on trade and bartering long before money and a currency was invented.

I keep preaching that if western civilization is to survive without going back to the Stone Age the nuclear and extended family system must be rebuilt. Nature's supreme law Of "Natural selection" uses a survival need to determine what exist or doesn't exist. If anything doesn't have a survival need it will slowly cease to exist.

The nuclear and extended family system will slowly cease to exist because the welfare state takes away its survival need. To sum it up, sure, the economy leg of the four legged survival stool is important, but far more important for human survival is the other three legs of the survival stool because every economy is going to collapse, it is only a matter of when.
NEW ENTRY ENDS

IDEOLOGY DISRESPECT IS REAL REASON FOR USA ECONOMIC FAILURE!
12 JUNE 2011, 1435 HOURS, NEW ENTRY.
There are only two major things that are going to save the USA economy and western civilization, I don't care what the eggheads and learned economist tells you. Those two things are a genuine free market place and a strong nuclear and extended

family system, which today both are in shambles.

We have a provider welfare state and it is impossible for the USA government to continue carrying that financial burden any longer. And anybody dumb or economically ignorant enough to think that it can be continued doesn't deserve freedom. In some of my other articles I have drawn a blue print on how to accomplish the task of rebuilding our nuclear family system and fixing the economy, which will be almost from scratch.
NEW ENTRY END.

IDEOLOGY DISRESPECT IS REAL REASON FOR USA ECONOMIC FAILURE!
Ideology is not built on what I think, you think, or what anyone else thinks, it is based on what has been proven by trial and error for over 5000 years of civilization. We know that the Ideology of socialism has never been proven to work successful, yet, it just won't go away and people keep coming up with a new twist on the same failure system.

We also know that a genuine true "Free market place" ideology that allows free competition has never failed to over produce, yet, the powerful always runs away from it, I believe it is because of its harsh discipline, it hinders favoritism and who you know, if you don't produce you are gone! The thing that sets me apart in economic terms from the eggheads is our views on ideology.

The egg heads are schooled and believe that man can successful manage an economy with fact and figures alone, I don't believe that is possible except within the bound of ideology. We know without a doubt that the "Free market place" works, but why? I believe the main reason why it works is it allows nature's supreme law of "Natural selection" to weed out excuses, inefficiency, and waste.

In economic terms you can call that law the "Invisible hand" or whatever but that is the real master of every economy. Sure, for 80-100 years almost any system may work, then it's Katy bar the door, and that is where we are at today. The egg heads think they can save the USA economy with all kinds of schemes and government controls, but I'm here to tell you it ain't gonna happen.

The best thing the government can do is get the hell out of the way and let a genuine true free market place work its magic. Human survival can best be described as a four legged stool, and the "Free market place" ideology is only one leg of that stool. The

first leg and most important one in my view
is the nuclear and extended family
ideology leg of that stool.

Ever since the dawn of history there has
never been a society that survived long term
without a strong nuclear and extended family
system, which the welfare state has
almost completely destroyed in the African
American community. The third leg of the
four legged survival stool is every society
must have a strong religious and moral code
in place to protect future generations;
otherwise no one will give a damn about
anything except themselves in the now.

The fourth and final leg of the stool is a
society must have adequate back up
bartering
capacity through many small farmers and
home gardeners in case the economy
collapses. Like life itself everything must have
a collapse or rebirth cycle after a period
of time or moral decay and every other kind
of inefficiency and waste will get too big
and choke of survival.

Because of our welfare state the USA simply
doesn't have enough people growing
food and that means millions of people are
going to starve when this global economy
collapses, no one know when but everything
must have a collapse or rebirth cycle to
exist.

The reason why man can't run a successful economy with facts and figures alone is because there are simply too many variables many of which are subjective, such as whose back is being scratched or who is under the desk and on and on.
SIRMANS LOG: JUNE 10, 2011, 1817 HOURS

LATE ENTRY: 28 JUNE 2011, 1200 HOURS
A PERFECT EXAMPLE OF WHY ONLY NATURE CAN DEAL WITH TOO POWERFUL ANTI-SURVIVAL FORCES IS THE RECENT NEW YORK LAW ALLOWING SAME SEX MARRIAGES.
There is something called a survival instinct that discipline and struggle instills in one which results in wisdom. Anyone with an ounce of wisdom by instinct alone will know that same sexes don't produce offspring and will ultimately lead to human extinction.

Yet, very few care or recognize that as a moral threat or for that matter even know what the hell a moral threat is. No problem, y'all. And the beat goes on. Whoa, what about Christian outrage? Oh, that, they are all out to lunch, y'all. And the beat goes on.

A moral threat is anything that threatens the

unborn and future generations. A moral threat may not be as immediately as a physical threat but given time the result will come to the same conclusion, human extinction.

The main purpose of a religion in the first place is to safeguard and protect morals; if I want a meeting place just to socialize I can do that in a dance hall.
LATE ENTRY ENDS.

GUARANTEED WEIGHT LOSS & CONTROL PROGRAM ANYONE CAN DO! JUST TWO STEPS ANYONE CAN DO: STEP 1. NO SNACKING BETWEEN MEALS. STEP 2. NO GOING BACK FOR SECOND HELPINGS, (first set out everything you plan to eat before starting, then no going back for anything, period.)
* ALL MEAL TIMES SHOULD BE A MINIMUM OF 3 1/2 HOURS APART.
* NO EATING OR DRINKING ANYTHING BETWEEN MEALS EXCEPT WATER AT ANY TIME.
* EXCEPTIONS MUST BE MADE FOR EMERGENCY AND SPECIAL CONDITIONS: Such as when sick, extremely tired or exhausted, special social occasions & celebrations, or any other special event.
* This program was conceived by self-made great Writer/Publisher/Philosopher/Inventor

Freddie L. Sirmans, Sr. and is offered to you and hopefully it will be helpful in some way. *Anyone that can't wait 3 1/2 hours from one meal to the next deserve to be fat sloppy and happy!

Writer's opinion on the epidemic of excessively over weight children:
To all parents your Child's eating habit and weight control is your responsibility. If your child is excessively obese it is your fault, not the tooth fairy or anyone else. A child is sort of like a blank slate and their access to food is under your control as a parent with few exceptions.

Real love is unselfishly doing what is best for the child, not being weak and irresponsible by catering to your own need to be loved by your child. A child is a separate human being that needs to be prepared to one day stand on his own, but irresponsible parenting in my view is more of an epidemic than obese children.

DIABETES HELPFUL HINTS
Every diabetic should read labels and keep count of the amount of carbohydrates consumed. Carbohydrates are really what determine ones blood sugar level. If carbohydrates can be kept down to around 50g per meal it will go a long ways in controlling ones blood sugar level.

Meats and fats without anything added like sauces and gravies don't contain carbohydrates. Most leafy vegetables and others like greens beans, broccoli, cauliflower, and sweet peas average around 15g per 1/2 cup. It is the big 5 that can be enjoyed but really need to be kept under control, they are bread, rice, potatoes, pasta, and artificial sweets.

One should always let his/her doctor know what vitamins, mineral, or any supplements one is taking. So, in case one wants to try diet first in controlling ones diabetes there are a couple of minerals that may help. They are Chromium Picolinate and Cinnamon capsules. Also, every diabetic must have a home tester to monitor his/her blood sugar level, plus a home blood pressure tester if you are taking blood pressure medication.

My healthy eating priority formula: Eat, fresh and raw when possible, cooked fresh, cooked frozen, and lastly cooked canned. However, as a rule eating food properly cooked is always safer in my view. I'm not a trained medical professional in any way; I'm a self-made writer and hope my limited knowledge will be helpful to someone in some way.

NEW TRAILBLAZING BREAKTHROUGH WEIGHT LOSING PROGRAM!

By Freddie L. Sirmans, Sr.

This weight control program I have just developed is truly a break through; because for the first time in my life of 68 years I feel I have dominant control over my compulsive overeating.

Anyone familiar with my writing knows that I have a super strong belief in "positive thinking" to change behavior. To those that don't know what positive thinking is, I will explain.

It is a technique to change behavior; take a phrase or quote and repeats it over and over to yourself. It doesn't need to be repeated aloud.

However, to be effective it must be repeated at least fifty or more times every day. The more times it is repeated the faster it will work because it is the repeating process itself that breaks through to the subconscious.

The quote to repeat is: **"A little bit of food is enough for me;" through God which strengthens me (The through God which strengthens me part is optional).** It may take as long as a year or longer to fully kick in, and bear fruit, but if one doesn't quit the repeating process is guaranteed to get results.

Just keep repeating the quote to yourself at least 50 times or more every day, and never quit until your goal is reached. God will make a way out of no way. Mighty forces will come to your aid. It will work if one doesn't quit.

A word of advice about changing eating behavior, it can be done but it is not a simple or easy matter. The only guarantee is to never stop repeating the quote because fat cells don't like being starved. One may start craving sweets and wanting to eat everything in sight and feeling the quote is a waste of time all to get you to quit repeating the quote.

The body cells in cahoots with the mind will play all kinds of tricks to get you to quit but in the end you will reach your goal if you stay with it and never quit. It is like breaking in a wild horse.

The wild horse is going to buck and try everything in its power to throw you off but if you can hang on and ride it out you will obtain your goal. The reason it is so hard to lose weight is your body cells in cahoots with your mind will use reward and punishment against you.

The punishment of hunger may seem much more severe. And at the same time the good taste of food may seem much more rewarding. However, in the end the mind must try to carry out any image constantly presented to it.

WEIGHT BATTLE BEGINS!
I, Freddie L. Sirmans, Sr. have decided to share with my readers the
inner working of my mind out loud as I try to discover secrets on how to lose weight.

The tactics I try may not work; still, I decided to share with my readers as I plot my strategy on defeating my sometimes-overpowering compulsive overeating habit.

WARNING: I check with my doctor before trying anything new or stressful.

Positive thinking has been proven to change behavior when the same quote or phrase is repeated to oneself at least 50 times or more every day. The more times it is repeated the faster it works. The quote to repeat is: **"A little bit of food is enough for me;" through God which strengthens me (The through God which strengthens me part is optional).**

Positive thinking is a slow process, sometimes it can take 6 months to a year or even longer to fully kick in.

Just as our main survival responses are fight or flight, reward or punishment are the main responses that control our behavior. Nothing in nature is all good or all bad; it is a matter of degree and balance.

The reward of pleasure and good taste is necessary to make sure we eat, but the balance arm of too much is not kicking in with compulsive over eaters like me.

So, maybe through "Positive thinking" an artificial overriding braking system will work. There is nothing to lose but weight.

The problem of overeating starts from eating when not hungry for whatever reason. Once the "Don't eat when not hungry" response is shoved completely out of the picture, for some, overeating becomes a compulsion.

Then any attempt to limit the amount and push away from the table is looked upon as a cruel punishment and taking away a deserved reward.

The key is to realize that too much food intake is really a punishment of survival instead of just a harmless too much of a good thing reward.

10 NOVEMBER 2010, 1853 HOURS: Last entry.

19 NOVEMBER 2010, 1708 HOURS: New Progress reporting my quest to discover secrets on losing weight I will use the

"Positive thinking" technique on myself to gauge my progress.

From my previous entry I established that it is reward or punishment that controls all normal human behavior. Also, I established that once the
"Don't eat when not hungry" response is ignored enough the inner mind then see all eating including over eating as a reward. Then no amount of eating is viewed, as punishment and stomach capacity becomes the only stopping point.

Now, the first strategy I'm going to use is to set eating rules followed by punishment for every infraction of those rules.

Rule number one: I'm going to decide on what weight I plan to get down to and list it on paper. My current weight is 252LBS and my goal weight is 195LBS.

Rule number two: I'm going to limit all meals to one helping, no second for anything. I try to make it a habit to bless the food before each meal that signals the start of the meal and after that no going back for seconds. Then nothing else can be added.

Rule number three: Set everything I plan to eat before me before I start, after that no going back for seconds. Once I start

eating and notice something I really like and want, I'll just remember I can have it my next meal three and one half hours later.

Rule number four: No snacking between meals.

Rule number five: No meals will be eaten at less than three and one half hours intervals. All rules and conditions may be waived only if I'm sick or doing extra strenuous work.

Rule number six: Unlimited amounts of water are permitted at all times, but Juices, sodas, or high protein drinks are permitted not less than three and one half hours intervals

Snacking is something that needs to be discouraged: Contrary to what people think most people are not overweight because of extra large over powering meals, but because of snacking on junk foods and sweets, especially kids.

Rare exceptions only:
* Allow for an occasional glass of wine or drink in a social situations.
* Allow for an occasional sweet treat or snack between meals with someone special in a social situation.
* Allow for a cola whenever indigestion

calls for it
* my being a diabetic allow for a very
small snack at anytime there
is must need.
* On special occasions after 3 1/2 hours
a very small snack is
allowed to extend time for a more
comfortable regular meal.

Remember reward or punishment is what shapes all behavior and that includes eating behavior. So, that means if I break one of my own eating rules I must punish myself for the infraction.

Whoa, hold on, I'm not talking about any harsh, cruel, or diabolical like punishment, but still, a message must be sent that rule breaking will not be tolerated.

The punishment stick I'm going to use on myself is going to be the
punishment of fasting limited to juices, sodas, high protein drinks, or
water but absolutely no food.

All punishment will be limited to a minimum of 4 hours up to a maximum
of 24 hours. I'm going to assign a set punishment for certain infractions
for now and may add more later.

SET PUNISHMENTS:
(1.) Punishment for all rule violations

**except snacking: 24 hours
of fasting limited to juices, sodas, or
high protein drinks at not
less than three and one half hour
intervals. I can drink water
anytime, but absolutely no food for 24
hours.**

**(2.) Punishment for breaking the "No
snacking" rule: 3 1/2 hours
of fasting limited to water only but
absolutely no food.**

Here is the skinny on enforcing punishment for rule violations: This is something that must be enforced or else abandon this whole thing right now. That is because I have challenged my inner mind for dominance over my compulsive overeating habit and if I don't follow through with enforcement, my inner mind will come roaring back with a vengeance.

This is something I must never; never start or it will end up punishing me with much more extra weight gain unless I'm prepared to follow through on my punishment rules. My inner compulsions will reassert its dominance and take revenge if I become weak and fail to enforce all of the rules I set out. I hope you get the picture, messing around with something like this is not for the weak and goodie, goodie two shoes type, this is all about dominating or being dominated.

I may start craving sweet and wanting to eat everything in sight and end up gaining weight and eating far more than ever. That is why any serious major change in behavior is always going to cause some temporary stress.

I've decided to start repeating my latest positive thinking quote **"A little bit of food is enough for me;"** through God which strengthens me (The through God which strengthens me part is optional). Also, you keep checking I plan to make at least monthly progress reports.
19 NOVEMBER 2010, 2130 HOURS: Last entry

21 NOVEMBER 2010, 2025 HOURS: New progress report. Unlimited amounts of water are permitted at all times but juices, sodas, and high protein drinks are permitted only at no less than three and one half hours intervals.

There is no restriction on the amount of juices, sodas, or protein drink consumed at a time. Also, there is no set amount of meals per day, but no meal or drink is permitted to be served at less than three and one half hours intervals.

WARNING NOTE: Remember, I have the right and power to set or change the

rules anytime I want to, but, by God whatever rules that I list on paper must be obeyed and enforce to the tee or I suffer the consequences.

If I'm not willing to punish myself for every rule infractions I must
abandon this program this minute otherwise my inner mind is going to get revenge on me with much, much more weight gain for challenging it in the first place.

WEIGHT PROGRESS REPORT: Goal weight 195LBS
STARTED WEIGHT------------------**252LBS**
November 2010--------------------**250LBS**
December 2010--------------------**247LBS**
January 2011----------------------**245LBS**
February 2011---------------------**244LBS**
March 2011------------------------**239LBS**
April 2011-------------------------**240LBS**
May 2011--------------------------**238LBS**
June 2011-------------------------**237LBS**
July 2011--------------------------**236LBS**
August 2011----------------------**230LBS**

I'M ONE THAT SUFFERS FROM DIABETES!
So, I decided to write the very basics of understanding diabetes. They call it sugar diabetes and the old folks used to just say he/she "Got sugar." However, that is true, but that kind of talk can be misleading and doesn't tell the whole story.

The real story is carbohydrates are what determine the level of sugar in the blood, not just sugar and sweets. Yet, most people still automatically think of just sugar and sweets as the big bad boogie man that must be avoided at all cost.

The fact is sugar or sweets are only one type of carbohydrate. Things like bread, pasta, fruit, and vegetables are all carbohydrates that turn into sugar for the body to use for energy. Also, another big factor that determines blood sugar levels is the speed at which a carbohydrate turns into sugar.

Some types of carbohydrates turns into sugar very rapid and others very slow. The pancreas produces insulin to keep too much sugar from getting into the blood, but a diabetic person doesn't produce enough insulin or fast enough to block rapid sugar producing carbohydrates, thereby allowing too much sugar to overflow into the blood stream. Type 1 diabetic's pancreas doesn't produce any insulin at all.

However, a diabetic can do a lot through diet to control blood sugar level by eating carbohydrates that turns into sugar very slowly like green beans, broccoli, and leafy vegetables. That way his lesser producing pancreas may be able to keep up and keep his blood sugar level within the normal range.

The diet first method along with taking the mineral chromium picolinate may work for some, but, never try any method without first checking with a doctor and having a home testing kit to monitor ones own blood sugar level at all times.

Keeping all carbohydrates below 50g per meal will definitely help control blood sugar levels. Practice reading labels for the totally amount of carbohydrates per serving.

For us to live our bodies must get energy from the foods we eat. Our bodies breaks down the foods we eat in three ways, they are carbohydrates, proteins, and fats.

Proteins and fats alone don't turn into sugar or raise blood sugar levels as long as no gravies, sauces, or anything else is included. In fact some carbohydrates are high in proteins such as beans and nuts.

But, **for some unexplained reason fats tends to hinder blood sugar levels from dropping from whatever level it is at the time, otherwise without fats it tends to drop like a rock.**

The body prefers and will always choose the sugar from carbohydrates first to get its needed energy, then as second choice it will turns to proteins for energy.

NOTE: I am not a trained health care professional in anyway, but with my limited knowledge I decided to write this article anyway, I can only hope that I have been helpful to someone in someway. God bless you all.
SIRMANS LOG: 3 DECEMBER 2010, 1841 HOURS.

A QUICK BRIEF CONDENSE GUIDE
It ain't what you eat its how much you eat. Moderation is always
the key.

The two main things that make and keep most people fat are
going back for second and eating between meals.

Anyone that can't wait three and one half hours between each
meal is just plain greedy, selfish, and spoiled like a little kid.

My first rule is to first set a goal weight.

(1.) At meal time set out everything you plan to eat while no
overeating compulsion is controlling your mind and you can think
rational, then after the first bite no going back for seconds.

(2.) Don't eat or drink anything at less than
three and one half
hours intervals except for a celebration or
special occasion.
However, water may be consumed at
anytime.

Just do these two things and you will obtain
your goal weight?

THE MANGANESE FACTOR:

As a diabetic certain foods plays a big role in
my controlling my
blood sugar level. One should make it a
practice to read food
labels. It is carbohydrates that determine
blood sugar level more
than anything else.

The big five starches rice, bread, potatoes,
pasta, and bread along
with sweets are the highest in carbohydrates.
The foods lowest in
carbohydrates are leafy vegetables, broccoli,
cauliflower, green
beans, etc.

Meats and fats without gravies or sauces
don't have
carbohydrates and won't drive up blood sugar
levels, but fats do
have a tendency to keep blood sugar levels
from dropping.

Food also contains vitamins and minerals.
And there is one trace
mineral that I have noticed tends to drive my
blood sugar level up.
I don't know about anyone else and I have
never read or done any
research on it.

All I know is when I eat food that contain this
trace mineral it
drives and keeps my blood sugar level up a
lot higher. The trace
mineral I'm talking about is manganese, so,
when I see it on a
food label I make sure I keep my portions a
lot smaller.

Again, I'm not a trained medical professional
in any way, I'm just
sharing my limited knowledge and hopefully it
may help someone
in some way.

THE RANTING OF A LUNATIC, YOU DECIDE?

Like I've said before, I understand how an
economy truly works as well as anyone I
don't care how many degrees they have. And
I'm here to tell you I believe all of the recent
spending cuts are going to do is speed up the
demise and day of reckoning of our welfare

state.

I don't want to be right on this, almost no one believes me anyway, so, let everyone just continue on his or her merry way. Sure, before the "New deal" and even on up to the late seventies cutting government spending would have reduced the size of government.

But, not any more there are far too many social programs waiting to kick in and over compensate for every spending cut advantage thereby vastly growing big government even more with an ever increasing dole population.

Plus, today this welfare state has grown into this super beast that has all but destroyed our nuclear and extended family system and all of the rest of the pre "New deal" survival infrastructure.

It is not too late to save individual freedom and the last bastion of true freedom in the world today, but the options are down to survival or getting big government out of its super provider role.

Until big government is de-clawed out of its all power super provider role no political party or anything else is going to keep it from spending this nation into total doomsday oblivion.

I try not to promote self in my writing but I do want to stress a point, I have the depth, the wisdom, the perspective, and the awareness that very few have, and I believe beyond a shadow of a doubt that these spending cut are going to put this great nation in a do or die situation.

Caution, get ready for mass unemployment almost beyond the imagination. Caution; get ready for the dole population to increase like never before because the liberals, the head of household women, and the countless special interest groups are going to start screaming bloody murder about these spending cuts affect on social programs.

And I will be agreeing with them, because in a welfare state it is unfair to cold turkey throw people to the wild without providing a lifeline. The nuclear family system has been ripped to threads by the welfare state and that have left masses upon masses of people that have never been conditioned to survive without the government dole.

Abandoning these people is like setting a tame animal loose into the wild, it would have little chance of survival. The politicians will not be able to resist it; a tax raise will be imposed on the fewer and fewer surviving businesses thereby driving the final nail in the coffin.

I, Freddie L. Sirmans, Sr. have thrown out a survival lifeline and it is being completely ignored, my view is a drowning man shouldn't be choosey. No one will take me serious; I know the eggheads will never listen to my great wisdom because I don't have a Yale degree or for that matter even any college degree.

However, I must do my duty and pass it on regardless. Here is my survival solution, it is no cure all, and it is only a mean to prevent a total meltdown with millions upon millions starving to death in the USA.

No one will win but we will survive. The first order of business is the death grip the welfare state has on our nation's economic throat must be broken before there is any chance of this nation surviving with freedom intact.

If the nation doesn't have the will or guts to take this drastic step then you might as well stop reading, my solution is then out of the question. I will lay out three steps to prevent the total meltdown of the USA economy.

(1.) To break the welfare state death grip the first thing that must be done is the "Minimum wage" must be completely eliminated because in free market place economics terms that is like a vehicle with no reverse or a water heater with no pop off valve.

(2.) In the USA the nuclear family system is almost totally destroyed from lack of need because of the welfare state, that means the government must never abandon these people without giving them a lifeline until the nuclear family system is restored.

Sure, these people must be helped but government must never give anyone free money on an individual basis, because that is what destroys the balance between the merchant and the consumer. That is what causes inflation and is the cause of the out of control inflation we have today.

(3.) Under current conditions the government must provide help to the poor and disadvantage but never by giving out unearned money on an individual basis. Government must provide temporary government commissaries, housing, and clinics to keep people alive until the nuclear and extended family system is rebuilt in this nation.

Also, to keep government spending from contaminating the free market place some type of script or tokens must be use for those qualifying for government help. A true free market place economy has never failed in the history of civilization because nature's law of "Natural selection" weeds out inefficiency. It is only through government interference instead of just collecting the taxes that kills every economy.

The nuclear and extended family system is how people survived for over 5000 years before the "New deal" came along and created this super welfare state beast, and there is not enough money in the whole wide world to keep this beast fed.
SIRMANS LOG: 9 APRIL 2011, 2029 HOURS.

Economic wise, all of the spending cuts and taxes remaining the same are going to do is take a smaller pie out of the oven.

The only thing that is going to stop this runaway economy is booting the welfare state out of the all-powerful social and family provider role, by eliminating the minimum wage as a first step. After the government first establish community wise only emergency kitchens, shelters, and clinics

A CURRENT EVENT ISSUE:
I saw on TV where two small minority talk radio hosts are going all out to try to destroy the biggest talk radio show host. They say it is in the name of protecting the public from race baiting. I think what they fail to understand is what free speech is truly all about.

Free speech is not just about what we agree with and want to hear, it is more about protecting that speech we disagree with and don't want to hear. Hell, I feel anyone that genuine love and accept his or her own true self-identity will not feel threaten by every so called race baiting insensitive comment, because what is good for the goose is good for the gander.

I am already secure on who I am and stuff like that to me is like water off a ducks back. The key is to love and accept all people even if it is not returned, especially those of your own race who look like you.

No one is perfect and everyone has flaws, even if they don't show. Many, many people will totally disagree with everything I just said; still I have a right to say it under the five freedoms listed in the 1st amendment to the constitution of the United States of America.

SIRMANS LOG: ON THIS 69th PEARL HARBOR ANNIVERSARY DECEMBER 7, 1941, I WRITE THIS TODAY 1201 HOURS.
23 NOVEMBER 2010 1527 HOURS:

New update on airline search techniques.
I think the airlines, the workers, and all involved are trying their level best to make

the best of a bad situation and keep the flying public safe. Then on the other hand you have this negative constant drumbeat by much of talk radio and other armchair quarterbacks second-guessing the best safety possible for the American flying public.

What this could end up doing is forcing the management into lesser security. Then guess what? Who do you think may end up taking much of the blame and heat if a plane ends up being blown out of the sky? Need I say more?

A CURRENT EVENT ISSUE: 22 NOVEMBER 2010, 2205 HOURS:
New comment on airline search technique.
I think a few people are trying to keep a bandwagon going. Being patted down is not new, you go back over 40 to 50 year before modern metal detecting devices and it was not uncommon at all for some night clubs to do pat downs.

Its been over 50 years when I was a young man I along with everyone else was patted down before enter a night club and no one raised any hell about it. No court is going to touch this with a ten-foot pole, because then they would be responsible for what ever happens.

The people raising so much hell don't have to

answer for anything if a plane is blown up.

THE AIRLINES SEARCH TECHNIQUE!
Let me get this out of the way first, having the pilots go through the same search technique is nonsense in my view. However, folks if not the strict search technique, what is your solution?

Right now the same folks pissing and moaning the loudest will be the same ones complaining the loudest if their loved ones are on a plane that blows up. Come on folks, no one has a gun to anyone's head telling them that they gotta fly.

Take your voyage by ship or other means if it's that bothersome. What are you going to tell your urologist if you have a medical problem, it is the same with the intent not to be sexual in any way? At the rate of technology advancement today a better remedy should come about very soon.

But, until that happens, I say fly safe and live because it is not about any one individual. I seen a lady on TV get all angry and rebellious, but, she could never come up with a real or better solution, which is the case with most of the get on the bandwagon complainers.

The vast majority of the people doing that type of work dislike the technique as much as you, but these people have family to feed. And his or her management has a responsibility to keep everyone alive. Talk is cheap.

F L SIRMANS, SR. PLEAS FOR DIVINE HELP! The thing about me that make my great thinking so awesome is it is not limited in any way; it has no borders or boundaries.

I have never been to economic school or taken any such classes! I don't know what is not supposed to work! Almost all of my thinking is original; it is raw and creative from the core! Plus, my thinking takes in vastly more than the economic one leg of the whole survival stool.

I'm more of a deep thinking philosopher that sees the whole survival stool and how the economy fits into the grand design. There are infinite variables in an economy many are subjective, which makes it impossible to be managed by man even with a super computer.

What actually runs every economy no matter the type of government is nature's supreme law of "Natural selection." Sure, almost any liberal bleeding heart do good economic system may work for 80-100 years, but, then the consequences of ignoring nature's supreme law of "Natural selection" catches up.

And then someone is gonna pay in blood, sweat, or tears. The nuclear and extended family system is the foundation of human survival. And is protected under nature's supreme law of "Natural selection." So, when the welfare state for all practical purpose destroyed our nuclear and extended family system the consequences is going to make us pay dearly, hopefully we will survive as a nation.

I'm paraphrasing when I say someone complained that democracy was a terrible form of government but is still the best government known to man. That is why I often wonder why is it so hard for nations to use an economic ideology that has never failed and have proven to always work time and time again.

It will always produce an over abundance of everything. That ideology is: "Allow free competition and let the free market place work." I think the real reason is governments just love power and the ability to control too much. Another cold hard fact on that matter is:

It is impossible to "Have free competition and a free market place" with government finger all in the pie. The more government gets involve the less of a free market place you will have. When government sets a minimum wage, which is like a vehicle with no reverse and enacts every kind or regulation and mandate one can imagine that means our USA economy

doesn't even come close to being a free market place. That being the case, no one has to tell me that a total collapse is possible.

In the distance past a collapsing economy was something almost normal. It was just a rebirth or renewal. The strong nuclear and extended family system along with plenty bartering capacity would keep order until enough new growth kicked in.

We no longer have that safety valve anymore, western welfare states has just about destroyed that entire infrastructure. We no longer have a strong reliable nuclear and extended family structure anymore everybody is depending on our welfare state daddy.

Much of our moral and religious code has been reduced to what comes out of Hollywood. And we no longer have enough backup emergency bartering capacity in small farmers and home gardeners like what got us through the great depression.

This welfare state super beast has left this great nation with almost nothing in term of bare boned survival in time of crisis. We as a nation could face almost total chaos. GOD, I ASK IN YOUR NAME, SAVE OUR GREAT NATION! **SIRMANS LOG: 9 NOVEMBER 2010, 1830 HOURS**

IS WORLD TURMOIL THE HIDDEN HAND OF: A. FATE, B. DESTINY; C. GOD; D. ALL OF ABOVE?

I may be wrong but I have a different take on what is actually taking place in the Middle East. I think there may be a flaw in western thinking on what is really happening in the Moslem world.

In my view from what I see on TV western thinking doesn't have a clue as to what is actually the underline views and feeling with these people. Question, what is the first thing any organized group will do when it feels its survival is threatened?

The smart and wise thing to do is get back to the basics. So far western civilization has failed to do this and until this is done western civilization has no chance of survival.

I believe the Moslem world is addressing this problem and is trying to get back to their basics. Sure, the intellectuals and educated doesn't have that in mine but I assure you the masses are dead set on reestablishing Sharia law throughout the whole Moslem world in my view. And I predict that is where this whole movement is headed.

There are two sides to modern communications and the Moslem world doesn't like what they see. With modern computers, cell phones, and other communication they see the deadly moral threat of porn and other moral decay and they don't want this stuff invading their world.

You mark my word! I believe economic is a factor, but this is much more of a moral movement than anything else in my view. I also believe this moral issue is something the Christian faith has failed on big time.

In many ways a moral threat is much more dangerous than a physical or mental threat, but, after around 80 years of our liberal welfare state most Americans couldn't recognize a moral threat even if it slapped them upside the head.

Morality is the only thing that truly protects future generations. Morality is the only thing that holds a society together long term. Laws alone won't hold a society together long term, especially if no one respects or believes in the law.

Without morality it's back to the law of nature meaning the survival of the strongest and the fittest.

SIRMANS LOG: 26 MARCH 2011, 1017 HOURS. CURRENT EVENTS:

WISCONSIN STATE SENATE FILIBUSTER ANALOGY! 9 MARCH 2011, 1015 HOURS
Everyone knows that the United States senate has a tradition and long accepted form of a filibuster. But, now we have this new radical form of filibuster that has cropped up in the Wisconsin State senate that gravely concerns me.

Sure, I believe winning at all cost may win you a battle but something like this in the long run could threaten our republic form of government, then we the people all loses the war. God I ask in your name, save our republic form of government for my grand children and generation to come.

14 FEBRUARY 2011, GOVERNMENT SPENDING CUTS UPDATE:
Like I've said many times before, less than five percent of the USA population truly understands how an economy really works and that includes learned economists. They don't teach what I tell you in schools.

This nation has took the course of least resistance and allowed the liberals to create this monster size welfare state beast that has all but completely destroyed our once strong nuclear and extended family system.

Common sense should tell anyone that understands basic economics that mass government spending cuts at once are going to speed up the collapse of this welfare state by creating hoards of new dependents and mouths to feed.

What is truly needed is a back to survival basics, meaning a way must be found to rebuild the nations nuclear and extended family system and get back to a true free market place economy or as near as possible.

But, that can never be done with government taxing the hell out of businesses to kingdom come. I understand, but less than five percent of the general population understands that all profit originates with some type of trade or business transaction from the private sector.

And the sad fact is the heavy hand of government taxes and self-initiative killing regulations is drying up that profit generating well. And guess what? Government will dry up, too. The only way this great nation is going to be saved is through private enterprise.

Government must be voted back to its designated role in our free republic as the guardian and protector and doing only what the people can't do for themselves.

A nation cannot remain free and survive with government in the role of super family provider simply because without a survival need the two family household will soon disappear and so will the nation.

As a man of great supernatural wisdom I suggest we start the process by first completely eliminating the minimum wage and government must stop giving anyone free money on an individual basis. That doesn't include anyone working for government.

The government should help the poor and unemployed by establishing government run commissaries, houses, and clinics with the use of token only to qualify, then the free market will remain free not contaminated and inflated out of sight like it is now.

. Otherwise, in a welfare state any drastic government spending cuts is only going to mean a smaller pie to be shared by many more dependents and mouths to feed. Jesus wept. My God! I slam my hat on the floor! Lord help us! It is sad and hard for me to watch my beloved homeland commit economic suicide!

For several years I have been ranting and

raving at the top of my voice but it is like water off a ducks back. No one will listen and I'm totally ignored, what else can one do. This nation is on an unsustainable course leading to sure doom. But, what do we do? The conservatives are fixing to jump out of the hot water into the fire.

As I watch this so called conservative government spending cut craze go on as if it is some kind of fascinating game being played. Sure, this nation is headed toward doom and something definite need to be done but in my view economic suicide is not the answer.

Opinions are like a-holes with everyone having one including me. Just because someone is a learned economist doesn't mean he/she truly knows what the hell is going on. You keep believing the egg heads with their always toeing the government line with figures to support it and we all are gonna perish.

Don't believe anything just because I say it, but also don't dismiss anything I say when it is based on over 5000 years of tried and true civilization proof.

When I pound and pound away on the necessity of the nuclear and extended family system and the fact that a genuine free market place economy has never failed to produce an over abundance of everything you can stake your life on it.

No system of government has ever survived in the history of mankind without the nuclear family unit head of household filling the role as the provider.

That last statement lead to this truth, which I believe, is the root cause of America's economic and culture meltdown. And until this root cause is dealt with and corrected this nation will never survive as a free nation.

The root cause I'm referring to started with the "New deal" when the liberals seized the nuclear family provider role from the traditional male head of household and then government became a sugar daddy.

That one act did something to the African American race that even slavery couldn't do.

That root cause has almost completely destroyed the once proud and safe all black neighbor hoods. It has almost completely destroyed the once strong black nuclear and extended family system and community.

Proportional wise more African Americans babies are killed in the wombs than anywhere on earth. Also, approaching 80 percent of all African Americans babies are born out of wedlock.

Now, what do all of that have to do with America's economic problems? A lot, once government became a super sugar daddy family provider (and it is a sugar daddy provider because it has never enforced discipline or demanded qualification to receive free handouts) it has not only destroyed our economy it has rotted away our culture, too.

For all of these years conservatives have stood by and let the liberals grow this vast welfare state into a super beast. Now over 95 percent of the population expects government to always be there to take care of them if they need it. So, I think it is wrong for conservatives to snatch that false sense of hope from under these people without throwing them some kind of a lifeline.

I believe less than five percent of the population understand basic economic because all of these people think cutting government spending is going to reduce the size of government, wrong.

It is going to increase the size of government by increasing the government dole population. The only way to reduce big government when it is a welfare state is to reduce government's role as a family provider.

I have offered a great **suggestion** on how to solve the dilemma, because with a welfare state the more you cut government spending the more you put people out of work and increase government dependency.

Also, increasing the governments dependency population forces government to raise taxes even more on the businesses left standing thereby driving even more people out of work.

Government should never give out free money on an individual basis. Government should help the poor and unemployed by establishing temporary government run commissaries, housing, and clinics with the use of tokens only to qualify.

Government should never give free money and food stamps to anyone on an individual basis because that is what has destroyed our economy.

Government giving out free money on an individual basis destroys the balance between the merchant and the consumer.

So, when government gives the poor the money to pay the merchants higher and higher prices that allows the merchants to stay in business and keep prices high for everyone.

Then government raises taxes higher and higher on the merchants to provide care for more and more government dependents in a never-ending upward spiral. Lord save this great nation.

SIRMANS LOG: 10 FEBRUARY 2011, 2305 HOURS.

LIBERALS DARE CONSERVATIVES TO MAKE THEIR DAY, DO MASSIVE SPENDING CUTS!

01 FEBRUARY 2011, 0925 HOURS: UPDATE

The main reason I'm so against conservatives doing massive government spending cuts out of the blue is because the liberals with their welfare state has severely crippled private enterprise and nearly destroyed the once strong reliable nuclear and extended family system in this nation.

Before the "New deal" came along the people's survival depended on private enterprise and the strong reliable nuclear and extended family system and hardly anyone depended on government for their survival.

Balance is the key, social security was a good thing as a supplement for the handicapped, widows, and the elderly but everyone knows that balance is no longer the case.

Now, the liberals with their welfare state have created masses upon masses of government dependents and have all but destroyed our once strong nuclear and extended family system umbrella.

So, in my eyes it would be cruel and unfair for conservatives to snatch the rug from under these people before throwing them some type of lifeline.

The lifeline I have suggested is to stop all government free money handouts to anyone on an individual basis because that destroys the free market place and is what keeps driving prices higher and higher for everyone.

Once that is done establish temporary government commissaries, houses, and clinics that will require tokens only to participate, that way the national currency and the free market will stay pure and won't be contaminated with uncontrolled inflation.

So, I say give these people a lifeline first, next eliminate the minimum wage, then conservatives "Do your thing" cut taxes, spending and everything else to the bone, hurrah, hurrah...

30 JANUARY 2011, 1855 HOURS: UPDATE

I'm confused! I'm hearing that cutting government spending is going to increase jobs. I say poppy cock, hogwash, bull, nonsense; I beg your difference because I'm convinced that when you cut government spending you put people out of work.

There is no way of getting around that fact. Now, if you tell me you are cutting taxes then I agree that is going to increase jobs, but government spending, no way. If you do massive cuts in government spending that is going to put massive amounts of people out of work.

The question is what is going to happen to these people? Do these people find new jobs or do they greatly increase the government dole population. Obvious the dole population is going to increase because hardly anyone can find a job as it is.

If conservatives actually believe that massive cuts in government spending are going to increase jobs, then we are in more trouble than even I could imagine. Who am I, but I must say unless somebody starts taking me serious and listening to some of my ideas this run-a-way economic train is definite going to crash and burn.

I'm not totally against cuts in government spending, but you can't ignore the facts. When you cut government entitlements that cut their administrative staff and if it includes less money going to recipients, too, anyway you look at it that is money that won't be available to retailers.

As long as more than forty percent of the American people depend on the government as their super provider they will never vote to bite the hand that feeds them.

So, anything conservatives do that don't work to take back the provider role for the individual family unit where it had been for over 5,000 years until the "New deal" came along is a waste of time.

MY Warning to the Tea party and conservatives, if you do massive government cuts in spending it's going to backfire on you. The first thing is it won't stop job loss or truly control government spending it will only be committing political suicide.

Remember, the unemployment rate is already extremely high and massive government cuts all at once is going to mean even more massive unemployment. Sure, something can be done but that ain't the way to go about it.

Conservatives must get all of their ducks in a row first; I will get to my suggested way to go about it later. If the conservative insist on plowing ahead with massive cut in government spending all it is going to do is put the liberals back in power.

They are the ones that overall caused the fix we are in today starting with the "New deal." Again you will almost never hear me mentioning a political party simply because there are a lot of under cover liberals in the Republican Party and almost vice versa in the Democratic Party.

I often refer to liberals as being shallow but you won't ever hear me referring to liberals as being dumb or stupid. Overall liberals are much smarter and intelligent than conservatives in my view, why do you think they were able to take over almost all of our colleges and universities and most of the institutions in this country.

But, in my view they are still shallow surface dweller that should never control the long-term destiny of a country. Once the "New deal" gave them the excuse to seize the social and family provider role for themselves they have never looked back, they kept almost absolute power for forty years.

They did it simply by giving the people what the people wanted at taxpayer's expense, which they are still doing to this day. And I don't think they know or care if that destroys character in the people and will bankrupt the country, I believe they feel to hell with country as long as it keeps them in power.

Anyone with an ounce of common sense knows to keep overspending like the government is doing is going to destroy this great nation. Still, do you know anyone with an ounce of common sense that believes with liberal in power they will ever control overspending, I don't.

So, it's very simple, if this great nation is ever going to be saved, the conservative will have to fight against all odds to do it. Saving this great nation is something a lot easier said than done because the shallow minded liberals have not only destroyed the economy they have created masses of dependent voter with a flawed do-for-me mentality.

If conservatives are going to save this great country it can't be done by taking away the only means the masses of government dependents has been conditioned to survive on without some guaranteed replacement.

That is why if the conservatives go ahead with massive government cut in spending its going to put many more out of work, and I will guarantee you they will be voted out of office even with people knowing something must be done about overspending.

Again, I will promise you as long as

government is in its all powerful role of social and family provider, government over spending will never be brought under control, the politics will never allow it because the liberals will see you in hell first before they will ever stop growing government.

I have already given the best conservative solution that I know of in the form of a suggestion. My suggestion is to **first run a test** in a large northeastern city to test the theory and work out any kinks.

The purpose of the suggestion is to stop government from giving out free money on an individual basis. That will stop government from subsidizing higher and higher prices thereby allowing poor people to pay their own health cost and other living cost.

I know most people will think my suggestion is not a good solution but it is. The main reason is the people dependent on the government to survive must know that they will not be abandoned with no food, shelter, warmth, or medical care.

That is what I meant by conservatives having all of their ducks in a row, conservatives must never do massive government spending cut before guaranteeing the poor and the unemployed a means to survive, but, they should never give out free money on an individual basis if the free market economy is to survive.

The poor and unemployed should be given token that can only be spent in temporary government run commissaries, housing, kitchen, and clinics. Then with government no longer giving out free money on an individual basis prices will have to drop to where the poor can pay for their own medical care and other cost or no merchants can stay in business.

I don't see any other way to political get past the liberals and save this great country's economy from crashing and burning. Temporary running government run commissaries, housing, kitchens, and clinics will cost money but that type of spending doesn't destroy the free market place and drive up consumer prices for everyone like what's happening now.

Then if the minimum wage is eliminated the economy can't help but boom. Sure, at first the liberals and the masses of government dependents will never accept something like this and there will be an outrageous outcry.

But, with a little time the majority population will come around, because it knows we definitely are on a course to doom. Even the conservatives might not be on board for this, but I have made my case.

Now, it is up to others to take it from here, I will guarantee you, you will never defeat the liberals with cold turkey massive government spending cuts, that is only going to get conservatives kicked out of office.
.
No one has to take my advice for anything just continue on your merry way, we'll see.
SIRMANS LOG: 27 JANUARY 2011, 0016 HOURS.

20 JANUARY 2011, 1144 HOURS.
JUST AN OBSERVATION:
On TV I see all of the pundits and talking heads from the left and the right trying to figure out Sarah Palin and why she is such a lighting rod.

They watch and weigh every word she speaks trying to find a clue to as to what makes her tick. The liberals are almost out of their minds with frustration, anger, and a host of other emotions, all for reasons they themselves can't give a logical reason for.

To me the core reason is very simple and very clear. I'll just cut through the chase and quickly give you the core reason. The core reason is not political. The core reason and drive behind all of this fuss is the liberal instinct.
.
The liberals by instinct see her as a deadly

moral threat, especially liberal women and to their progress. The liberals are in boot shaking fear that she will get some real power, but they will never admit that, they just keep say she don't have a snowball chance in hell of winning.

.

Most conservatives and other are mostly fascinated by the whole thing and can't understand why the liberals dislike her so much. Some people are for her only because the liberals hate her so much.

Ever since the "New deal" moral and spiritual values in the USA has been declining and is now to the point that liberals will stop at nothing to try to destroy any genuine high moral person in the political arena. And they are right to be fearful because their forty years of absolute rule or to rule at all in the future is going to become more and more remote.

That is because the once big three no longer has absolute control over all free speech news, thanks to the blogs; talk radio, and other alternatives.

.

Now the real truth is getting through to educate the people on the dire fix the liberals has put this great nation in. That is my one-man analysis on what is taking place with Governor Palin.

.

However, the liberals can never be counted out or taken for granted because they do have one powerful advantage over genuine conservatives. Hardcore liberal lions will stop at nothing to have their way providing they can legal get away with it.
.

Whereas, most hardcore genuine conservatives has moral and self-restraint boundaries. Most genuine conservatives are bound by self-respect for the truth, for the protection of unborn future generations, and other moral considerations that would never deter a die-hard liberal from delivering a knock out punch.
.

These people are almost unstoppable in obtaining their goals. The only thing that is going to stop the liberals and save this great nation from total doom is to educate the majority public. Otherwise the liberals are too shallow to recognize their sure path to self-destruction to themselves and to the nation.

18 JANUARY 2011, 1730 HOURS
JUST AN OBSERVATION:
If you sit down to a card game and stake someone to bet against you then you end up owing them a lot of money how dumb is that. Well, this really happened to our drunk on spending welfare state, unbelievable. Boo hoo, cry me a river.

UPDATE: 16 JANUARY 2011, 0850 HOURS.
SOUL SEARCHING OUT LOUD!

Why! Why! Oh Lord, why do I continue on with this, where do this drive come from to continue on writing. I'm not selling enough books to enrich myself; this is almost a curse to me, why! Why! Why...

I'm no fool I know 98 percent of the people disagrees with my views, especially completely eliminating the minimum wage. Still, for some reason beyond me I'm driven by some unknown energy or destiny to plod on.

Just maybe I can do even a small thing to aid in keeping millions upon millions from starving to death when this economy crash and burn. There are no guarantees in life and I know my views may be wrong.

But still, it is insane for this great nation to continue on a course that every wise man/woman knows can't be sustained. Even a fool knows you must try to stop a run away train (The economy) even if you fail, I only see more money printing and government spending.

Sometimes under extreme conditions requires extreme actions and I don't see that happening. I suggested a testing of the **"No**

<u>minimum wage"</u> in practice in a large northeastern city, mute was the answer.

I don't care what it takes this run away train economy must be stopped before it crashes and burns with possible 100 million people starving to death afterward, and they won't even run a simple little **<u>test</u>** that may show how to save millions of lives. shame on you welfare state and egg heads. I take a moment of silence, you think about it.

CURRENT EVENT OPINION: 16 JANUARY 2011, 0855 HOURS.
I SIT NEXT TO YOU, YOU SIT NEXT TO ME!

Hogwash! It never ceases to amaze me of the bold scheming of the liberal mind. Now, all of a sudden liberals want to get rid of all labels and sit next to the opposition.

Why now? Do anyone think they would have come up with this before the last election, I don't. I think all of this new good intention is just a tactic to confuse the public. Right now they know the liberal ticket is not the hottest ticket in town so why not hid in plain sight.

Sure, if this is a genuine goodwill effort to last over time no matter who is on top I'm all for it but I don't think that is the case. Please don't hate on me, I'm only one man with one view and I could be wrong.

CURRENT EVENT COMMENT: 12 JANUARY 2011, 2016 HOURS.
FREE SPEECH:

Everyone agrees that unnecessarily shouting fire in an open theater must be banned. But, going past something simple like that could come to no ending.

It could lead to being punished for coughing at the wrong time in the wrong place. No one can predict where it will all end if we go down this political correctness road. Liberals are not against free speech; they are just against speech that is not shallow and irresponsible like their own.

They are too shallow to understand that there is a much bigger world out there than their shallowness can see. Over a hundred years or so ago the only place you could find a liberal was from a rich family and maybe on a college campus.

Today, around eighty years after the "New deal" they are crawling out of the wood works and everywhere, they have completely taken over our great colleges and universities. I tip my hat to them, these are awesome people there is nothing they will not do to attain their goals.

With 20 percent or less of the total population

these good intention shallow super aggressive people for all practical purpose has taken over and spent and ran this great country into the ground since the "New deal."

They grabbed this awesome power by taking the course of least resistance and handing out free government goodies at taxpayer's expense.

That is something that plays to our very basic human instincts and its extremely hard for almost everyone to resist the easy life of government assured pleasure and comfort. But, now we are face to face with that age-old axiom, "There are no free rides in nature," someone always pays one way or another and it may be in blood, sweat, or tears.

Only now with the once big three no longer in complete monopoly like control of all free speech news has the vise like liberal death grip on this nation's throat begun to loosen.

Now real true free speech is finally getting through to the people, I can only hope it's not too late to save this great nation from economic collapse and total liberal destruction. Amen, praise be to God.

UPDATE: 10 JANUARY 2011, 1200 HOURS.

I'm not against government spending to help people in severe need, but, what I am against is the type of government spending since the "New deal" that have destroyed our economy, culture, and nation almost to the point of no return.

I don't have a problem with the government spending like crazy as long as it doesn't hand out money on an individual basis. Handing out money on an individual basis destroys the natural balance between the buyer and the seller or the merchant and the consumer that in turn ignites the inflationary spiraling that is causing this insane runaway economy we have today.

Government giving out money on an individual basis is like cancer it first attacks and destroys the free market place economy, then the nation's culture, and on and on until a hollered out shell of a nation is left.

I don't enjoy being a spoilsport, party pooper; raining on anybody's parade, or any other bad news metaphor. But, one thing about me is no matter what it is I'm going to face it head on.

I have faced dreadful almost unbearable things all of my life and found you always come out better in the end no matter the results. Even if you are wrong face your mistake and try again.

I don't think this nation's leadership is willing to truly face down the dire situation our economy and nation are in. And I think this great nation will be left unprepared when the bottom falls out which anyone with an ounce of economic sense know is going to happen.

UPDATE: 10 JANUARY 2011, 0813 HOURS.

Okay, okay if my "No minimum wage" is so insane and unworkable why not at the least run a test case and see what happens. After all I'm talking about the future survival of this great nation and we are a civilized people, who can be against running a test.

Why not select Detroit or any large northeastern city for a five-year "No minimum wage" test case and see what happens in practice. I suggest First grandfather clause in all existing conditions. But, once the test takes effect I suggest no new government cash be given out on an individual basis.

I suggest some of the acres and acres of vacant building be used as government run commissaries, clinics or whatever is needed on a community wise basis. I believe this nation need to start preparing no matter how small on what I and all wise men/women know is coming soon to this great nation.

JOBS, THAT ELUSIVE CREATURE GOVERNMENT IS TRYING TO FIND!

As a self-made writer, publisher, philosopher, inventor, and original creative thinker, I decided to weigh in here on the lack of jobs debacle.

The first misconception is the purpose of a business or to go into business is to provide jobs. The need and reason for a business is to enrich or create a profit for the owner or owners and providing jobs is only a byproduct.

That being the case government goal and aim should be to set policies that will allow businesses to make more profit not less. And at the very least not create mountains of red tape. Nature's supreme law of "Natural selection" that controls everything on earth is base solely on a "Survival need."

For anything to survive or exist any period of time there must be a "Survival need" for it to exist or it will crease to exist, and that includes jobs. It is very simple if a business truly needs more help or job seekers it will hire them, their main complaint or problem is finding qualified job seekers.

The main reason government is desperate in job promoting is all of the dependents the welfare state has created since the "New deal" is coming with pitch forks if the provider checks isn't delivered. Now I refer back to the broken record that I have been playing for many years.

The ultimatum is either we give up feeding the welfare state beast or the great USA perishes. There is no other way out, the financial burdens and cost is simply going to kill this economy.

I believe the government as a social and family provider since the "New deal' has grown into this financial beast that is impossible to feed, and it is now eating the great USA out of a house and home.

To not face this reality is insane, stupid, and beyond irresponsible, it is sheer madness. With my supernatural wisdom I have suggested a means to defuse this time bomb from causing a total collapsing of the world's global economy, but to no avail, I'm totally ignored and dismissed as a nut case.

Maybe millions upon millions live could be saved, but what can I say, I'm seen as just a nobody trying play on the world's stage. I believe and suggested that completely eliminating the minimum wage would provide a way back to sanity and slowly slow down this runaway welfare state economy, stop it and reverse back away from the cliff it is about to go over.

Then with over 5000 years of proven human survival evolution we can head in the direction of the strong nuclear and extended family system. That will allow the one breadwinner household to rebound and again lead to unsurpassed greatness for the land of the free and home of the brave.

What? Well, I'm waiting! I'm waiting for the eggheads to say how they are going to stop this runaway economy from going over the cliff to crash and burn! I'm waiting for anyone to offer a better solution than mine! Will some mature adult please step up!

I know no liberal is going to step up they are too shallow to see any survival threat until it is tearing down the front door. Sure, ultimately all survival is based on need, but, the bonus to life is what do we want and desire which can be manipulated.

So, a business may not need more employees but if it is going to lead to enough profit to make it worthwhile then greed will kick in. There is no greater motivating energy force on earth than greed.

Greed is the only force that can make a free people and a free market place produce more of everything than any one nation can use. And are the main reason communist government, socialist government, and any system that shuts down greed will fail unless there are abundance natural resources to sell.

Greed is like electricity very dangerous but when harnessed is the most powerful motivating energy force on earth. If the USA government truly wants to produce more jobs it first must eliminate mountains of red tape greatly relieve the tax bite to allow businesses to make enough profit to make growth worth the effort.

That and that alone will free up entrepreneurs then greed will take it from there and boom the economy. But, the real solution in the end must be to get the welfare state out of the social and family provider role it is now playing.

SIRMANS LOG: 8 JANUARY 2011, 1216 HOURS.

BRIEF UPDATE:
When government gives out money on an individual basis to the poor in the long run it is not helping the poor or the country.

What that is doing is destroying the free market place, which in time will hurt everyone and hurt the poor the most by driving the cost of living out of sight.

If the government truly wants to help the

poor without doing a lot of damage and in the end destroy the country, it should establish government Commissaries, government housing, government clinic, or even issue government token chips.

Doing it that way wouldn't destroy the free market place like government has been doing ever since the "New deal." Issuing food stamps is a no, no because that is technical the same as giving out money on an individual basis.

Government can spend like hell all it wants to as long as it doesn't give out money on an individual basis because that is the one thing that affects and destroys the free market place.

In a natural healthy economy there is a natural balance between the merchant and the consumer that keeps the cost of living affordable and under control. But, when government gets involve it is like someone putting his thumb on the scale.

There is no way a greedy merchant can decide to charge a higher price than his competition and stay in business without government involvement because not enough people already have the money.

Cry me a river, and the government think it is helping the poor by handing out money on an individual basis. So, even now as back then the eggheads ignore and dismisses everything someone like me may say, even if it makes totally good sense and is sound judgment.

Like I've said thousands of times the economy is just one leg of the four leg survival stool, as a supposition if the USA had all of the money it needed to spend on anything it wanted to it still wouldn't save us from total doom, because the welfare state has rotted away the core of this great nation, there is legal murder in the womb and sodomy is no longer a kept secret in the military.

Sodomy the same as abortion on demand are instinctually a threat to future survival in almost all cases. Understanding this fact is something that can't be taught, but anyone one with a strong survival instinct will automatic knows this without being told.

Remember, I don't make any rules I just happen to have a super strong survival instinct that recognizes inherent threats to survival, no matter what they are.
LAST ENTRY: 22 DECEMBER 2010, 0305 HOURS.

WELFARE STATE BEAST MUST BE STARVED OUT OF THE PROVIDER ROLE!

Hear ye! Hear ye! Hear ye! To any one within the range of my voice, unlike the liberals hiding their real intentions, my intentions are to try to drive the welfare state out of being an individual family unit provider.

I don't believe there is anyway this great nation can survive and be saved as long as our super welfare state beast is in the family provider role it now plays.

I think the family provider role should be returned back to the individual family unit, and government should stay with protecting and defending the nation and doing only that which the people can't do for themselves.

Our super welfare state beast has destroyed our culture to the point that we are living in the now, me first, what do I get out of it, I want mine, I want it all, screw future generations, It's just a fetus, gimmy, gimmy, and on and on.

Self-sacrificing for the long term good of the country and sometimes willingly giving up a right for wrong for the long term good of the country is almost unheard of with most of today's leadership.

I just want everyone to know that I think the destruction of our nuclear and extended family system was caused by our liberal induced welfare state, and it have placed this great nation at deaths door.

I blame almost all of it on our liberal induced welfare state starting with the "New deal." Their intent was not to destroy the country; their intent was to irresponsible grab power and keep it at all cost by handing out free goodies at taxpayers expense.

Sure, during hard and trying times the government has a responsibility to provide on temporary basis community wise only emergency kitchens, shelters, and clinics, anything more will in time take away the need for the nuclear and extended family system thereby destroying the nuclear and extended family system, which have happen in the USA.

The individual family provider role must remain in the hands of the individual family unit breadwinner for any nation or society to survive long term.

We as a nation has failed to safeguard our nuclear family unit which is nature's first law of human survival enforced by its supreme law of "Natural selection." There has never been a surviving society in the history of mankind without the nuclear family unit.

The process of "natural selection is chasing this nation down and closing in on us and we are gonna pay dearly for destroying our nuclear and extended family system, hopefully we will survive as a nation.

About me: It may be as much as 95 percent of the people will see me as a cold and uncaring monster, but, when the bottom falls out of this welfare state and we won't have a leg to stand on, I will be the hero, by then it may be too late.

I'm all about doing the greater good meaning the long term survival of the entire species, not just short term pleasure and comfort, especially to those that don't do anything to earn their keep. I'm human I have feeling the same as all people.

I take no pleasure in being disliked and frowned upon, but I believe I have been chosen by destiny to help save this great nation and I cannot and will not dialect my duty come hell or high waters. Long live the great USA.

When I say get rid of the minimum wage the first thing most people will think is, my God! And think businesses will be in a race to see who can pay the least amount in wages. The truth is no one knows because it is a natural selection process and a business still has to pay the best wages to get the best people.

Plus, that is only one side of the coin, the other side of the coin is no business can charge more than the poor can afford to pay and stay in business, that is unless the government gives the poor the money to pay whatever price a business may charge.

Getting rid of the minimum wage would severely limit governments ability to drive up prices for everyone when it pays the poor enough money to keep high priced merchants in business, otherwise the cost of living could never out distance what the poor man could afford. Right now the cost of living is far above what a one-breadwinner provider can afford.

The merchant has to charge higher and higher prices to pay higher and higher taxes, license fees, permit fees, and countless other government mandates even before any business profit is made. And the government keeps growing bigger and bigger needing even more taxes to be even a bigger sugar daddy in a no ending inflationary spiral. Even a moron should see the hand writing on the wall, but oh no, not a shallow minded liberal.

It is impossible for this system not to crash no matter what the eggheads say. While all of this has been going on since the "New deal" it has hollered out the foundation and culture core of this great nation and left us with no means to survive through hard times or a severe crisis.

SIRMANS LOG: 18 DECEMBER 2010,

0204 HOURS.

DETROIT IS A LIBERAL EXAMPLE THAT AWAITS US ALL!!!

There was never a minimum wage before the "New deal" and this nation have been around well over 200 years

I love liberals some of my best friends are liberals we all are human beings, some of us are very shallow and some of us has great depth.

More than anyone else the liberals complains about no jobs, kids don't have enough to eat, and on and on. But, they are shallow and don't have the depth to realize that practically all of these ills are the direct result of their liberal policies more than anyone Else's.

I just shake my head and realize these liberals are like spoiled kids; you can't dislike them for their shallowness. I'm more saddened than hostile at them, but this is not Child's play this is the real world that is being screwed up.

This is why I try so hard to educate people with my deep wisdom and sound judgment. Actually our whole society is at fault for being seduced and lulled so far astray from what reasonable men and women know is down the wrong path.

It is natural for everything in nature to take the course of least resistance including man, but, we are human beings with the ability to reason and we should know better.

We should know that the road down the course of least resistance leads to "Easy come easy go." We should know that the road down the gambling path leads to a "Something for nothing mentality."

We should know that any road leading away from a strong nuclear and extended family system leads to murder in the womb and leaving our young undisciplined and unprepared for survival. We should know that good times are not going to last forever.

This liberal created welfare state has just about destroyed our nuclear and extended family system, our once super strong religious and moral values, and any capacity to barter with many, many small farmers and home gardeners, we have in a sense ate our seed corn and drink our priming water.

Now, we have almost nothing in terms of surviving through hard times, I pity the fool. By putting all of our eggs and faith in one super welfare state beast we are almost done in terms of emergency survival.

Look at what the liberals has done to the once great motor city and practical all of the big northeastern cities. The liberals have run these cities almost totally unopposed for years and look at the result, but they are still blaming everybody else and his brother.

Liberal policies have driven away businesses, the middle class, and everyone else with the means to escape. With sensible policies Detroit city can be saved with all of those abandon building coming alive and booming. All it takes is getting rid of the national minimum wage.

The eggheads think I'm stupid and they are the one's that know it all. I say eliminating the minimum wage is our only hope. It is true no matter if nobody believes it but me. As long as I have the mean I will keep pounding and shouting to anyone who will listen to my drumbeat of junking the minimum wage.

I don't think it will but I know it could turn our whole economy upside down. The fact is we don't really have a choice if we want to survive as a nation; otherwise we will end up as a region in some world body.

Anyone with an ounce of economic sense knows the current system we have is going to collapse, no one knows the day and hour, but they know it's going to happen. They are in denial and will never admit it in public but I will and continue to do so, unless they shut me down.

I know I'm branded and seen as a nut case, so be it, I'm only writing what I truly believe, I don't know why I'm doing this, I feel it must be destiny, sometimes I feel like a driven man on a treadmill and can't get off. In fact I hate the limelight and is uncomfortable around most people, especially strangers.

If the minimum wage is gotten rid of there is nothing saying that businesses will pay lower wages. A true free market place which it would be without any forced wages up or down. That would create a natural balance.

Sure, the cost of living would have to come down but I don't believe it would drop like a rock. Very few people would work for a dollar an hour because you couldn't buy enough to make it worthwhile.

But, in time the cost of living and the buying power of the dollar would seek a reasonable balance, whereas right now the average salary is far too low to come close to meeting the cost of living. The cost of living would seek a level down where one head of household could provide for a whole family.

Everything including medical cost would seek a natural level down to where everyone could pay out of pocket. If a business wanted the best workers it would still have to pay the best wages.

Sure, I keep harping on getting rid of the minimum wage, but the truth is if we don't do it the whole system is going to collapse and millions upon millions are going to stave to death.

You don't have to believe me, just keep feeding our liberal welfare state beast and we'll all find out sooner than we think.

.

I believe anything that will starve the beast out of its all-powerful social and family provider role is a good thing and the only way to save the United States of America. Unlike the liberals I will never hide my true beliefs. **SIRMANS LOG: 14 DECEMBER 2010, 0021 HOURS**

THE IGNORANCE OF ATTACKING THE RICH!

I feel a need to weigh in again on this subject. I believe anybody that attacks the rich is ignorant on what makes a democracy work or is just no friend of freedom and democracy.

Attacking the rich is the first thing a future dictator will do because he knows the rich is the lifeblood that makes a democracy works.

There has never been and never will be a rich and prosperous country without a lot of rich people to bring it about.

Rich people are not the same as poor people with money; there is a world of difference in motivation and attitude. As a supposition if all of the money in this country were spread equally among the people, it wouldn't take but a few years for almost all of the money to be back in the same hands.

Entrepreneur's registers very high in altruism, which is especially true when rewarded properly. Now, at the very opposite end of the totem pole where you will find the most dead beats and cop-out losers, and if you just scratch a little below the surface you will almost always find a very selfish self-centered individual.

Any type of government or economic system that won't let a lot of people become rich is going to fail, unless it is blessed with a lot of natural resources. These liberals and masses of government dependents don't have a clue as to what truly made this country great.

Throughout all of the early struggles this nation's culture always remained intact until the "New deal" came along. That is when the Liberals seized the traditional nuclear family provider role for themselves, and it wasn't long after that the black man was completely kicked out of the house.

Since then the liberals has slowly created social program after social program that conditions masses upon masses of people not to feel personally responsible for their own survival. These people have come to believe that it always someone else's responsibility or fault for their survival.

What are they going to do when this government is broke and can't borrow any more money or continue printing so much phony money that our currency will soon have the same worth as monopoly money?

Now the liberals are going all out attacking the rich instead of being thankful for the rich that supplies them with a job, which dead beats will never do. What you see on the surface and out front is never what it really takes to be a super achiever.

That is just a fraction of what it takes, you don't know it, but while you are in your easy chair or recliner kicked back with a beer or watching your favorite movie or TV program, the super achievers are doing backbreaking work or toiling away 15, 16, or more hour's a day.

With very few exceptions rich and successful people truly work hard and earn the money they make. Meanwhile the welfare state and its hoard of government dependents think they have a right to take that money hand some back and spend the rest as they please.

Then they act like they are doing the rich and super achievers a favor by giving them back some of their own money. The fact is not the rich nor anyone is actually getting a tax cut it is just staying at the same rate it's been for the last ten years.

If the liberals and big spenders had the power they would without a doubt spend this country into total oblivion and regress us all back to the Stone Age. Then while dragging the women by their hair into caves they would still be yelling it's the republican's fault.

Like I have said many times before, when you create a situation where the rich can no longer keep or hold on to their money that is the beginning to the end of freedom and democracy. The rich is the glue that holds every democracy together.

Like a broken record I repeat, as long as government is in the role of super family provider that is the force and drive that propels it to stop at nothing to retain that power, that includes everything it can beg, borrow, and steal, to keep their God like power.

Government will never go back to just protecting the country both internally and externally and doing only what the people can't do for themselves. Anyone thinking that lowering taxes and cutting spending is going to control the growth of big government has got the cart before the horse.

No one must be listening, how many times I must say that nothing is going to stop the growth of government as long as it is in its social and family provider role. It must first be booted out of that all powerful social and family provider roles or it's always going to be an exercise in futility, period.

There is a reason why most of the world is dirt poor and will always be poor. The main reason is ignorant people just can't resist the crablike mentality, and in my view that is the main force that is driving and feeding this attack the rich self-destructive movement.

The only way to bring power back to the people and the states is to completely get rid of the minimum wage, with all of my supernatural wisdom I can't think of any other way to get the welfare state out of its all powerful super family provider role. **SIRMANS LOG: 10 DECEMBER 2010, 1924 HOURS**

THE END

To purchase:
Freddie L. Sirmans, Sr. Books
Website: www.FLSirmans.com

www.ingramcontent.com/pod-product-compliance
Lightning Source LLC
Chambersburg PA
CBHW072035190526
45165CB00017B/923